sundance™

LITTLE RED
READERS

MW00488763

Animal Babies

PETER SLOAN &
SHERYL SLOAN

A baby tiger
is called a cub.

A baby dog
is called a puppy.

A baby goat
is called a kid.

A baby sheep
is called a lamb.

A baby cow
is called a calf.

A baby horse
is called a foal.

A baby person
is called ... a baby!